LISTENING FOR GOD

THROUGH

HEBREWS

Lectio Divina Bible Studies

wesleyan
publishing
house

Indianapolis, Indiana

Beacon Hill Press of Kansas City
Kansas City, Missouri

ABOUT THE
LECTIO DIVINA
BIBLE STUDIES

Lectio divina, Latin for *divine reading*, is the ancient Christian practice of communicating with God through the reading and study of Scripture. Throughout history, great Christian leaders including John Wesley have used and adapted this ancient method of interpreting Scripture. This Bible study builds on this practice, introducing modern readers of the Bible to the time-honored tradition of "listening for God" through His Word. In this series, the traditional *lectio divina* model has been revised and expanded for use in group Bible study. Each session in this study includes the following elements. (Latin equivalents are noted in italics.)

- Summary   A brief overview of the session
  Epitome

- Silence   A time of quieting oneself prior to
  Silencio   reading the Word

- Preparation   Focusing the mind on the central
  Praeparatio   theme of the text

- Reading   Carefully reading a passage of
  Lectio   Scripture

- Meditation   Exploring the meaning of the Bible
  Meditatio   passage

- Contemplation   Yielding oneself to God's will
  Contemplatio

- Prayer   Expressing praise, thanksgiving,
  Oratio   confession, or agreement to God

- Incarnation   Resolving to act on the message of
  Incarnatio   Scripture

The Lectio Divina Bible Studies invite readers to slow down, read Scripture, meditate upon it, and prayerfully respond to God's Word.

CONTENTS

INTRODUCTION

How often our circumstances loom large in our own eyes. Obscuring our vision. Skewing our perceptions. Diverting our attention. Taunting us to turn away from what we know to be true. These temptations were common when the writer of Hebrews penned his words of admonition and challenge.

The content of this book (probably written between A.D. 65 and 70) leads us to infer that the unnamed writer was addressing Jewish followers of Christ who were so tossed about by persecution from Jews and Romans that they were tempted to return to the familiarity of Old Testament law and thus renounce the name of Jesus.

The antidote to this temptation can be found in Hebrews 12:2, "Let us fix our eyes on Jesus." Poring over this Epistle will help us do just that. It is replete with references to Old Testament passages that point to their fulfillment in the person and work of Jesus Christ. Its focus is on Jesus as God Incarnate, Son of Man, and Great High Priest who lives to intercede for us.

This rich letter shows how our Savior is working on our behalf today from His position at the right hand of God's throne. Its challenge to believers now, as then, is to focus on Jesus, stand firm in difficult days, and hold to the expectation of a greater day in heaven. "For we do not have a high priest who is unable to sympathize with our weaknesses, but we have one who has been tempted in every way, just as we are— yet was without sin. Let us then approach the throne of grace with confidence, so that we may receive mercy and find grace to help us in our time of need" (4:15–16).

I WILL PAY ATTENTION

Listening for God through Hebrews 1:1–2:4

SUMMARY

God created us to live in intimate fellowship. Adam and Eve experienced that kind of relationship with Him and each other until they sinned. Genesis 3 records the events. Satan came in the form of a snake and lied to Adam and Eve. He implied that God had misled them by telling them that sin would kill them. They chose to believe the snake and ate the forbidden fruit. Their distrust and disobedience has been passed on to the entire human race.

God's solution was to begin revealing the truth about himself to our fallen race. His prophets were the first ones to declare God's message. Finally, Jesus came as both the message and the messenger. Anyone who wants to know what God is like needs only to look at Jesus. By paying close attention to Jesus and His message, you will begin to experience the intimate fellowship with God you were intended to enjoy.

Silencio
SILENCE ✝ LISTEN FOR GOD

Stand with your hands extended in front of you, with your palms down. Release your worries into God's care. Then turn your palms up to receive God's word for you.

Praeparatio
PREPARATION ✝ FOCUS YOUR THOUGHTS

From what three persons are you most likely to seek advice?

To whose counsel are you most likely to pay attention?

What traits do these persons have in common?

Lectio READING ✝ HEAR THE WORD

The book of Hebrews appears to have been written to Jewish believers in Jesus who were tempted to turn back to their old religious practices. The author is not identified, but he obviously knew a great deal about Judaism. Hebrews read more like a sermon than a letter. Its theme is the superiority of Jesus. It challenges believers to follow Him faithfully. In this opening passage the author makes the clear assertion that we must pay attention to Jesus.

In this study text you will encounter the following terms.

Prophets: These were men and women who proclaimed God's message to His people, particularly in Old Testament Israel.

Glory: This word refers to the brightness and the weight of God's obvious presence. The Lord's glory filled the Tabernacle when Moses dedicated it (Exod. 40:34).

Angels: These spiritual beings are God's messengers and servants, who help His people. The author of Hebrews implies that they delivered the Law to Moses on Mount Sinai. So do Paul (in Gal. 3:19) and Stephen (in Acts 7:53).

Drift: This word is used also to describe boats or ships without an anchor. They simply float away with the waves.

With these concepts in mind, read Hebrews 1:1–2:4 aloud in unison.

MEDITATION ☩ ENGAGE THE WORD

Meditate on Hebrews 1:1–4.

The author contrasts the message of the prophets and the message of the Son. How was Jesus both the message and the messenger? What advantage does that give Him over the prophets? Why?

In what ways has God spoken to you? Which seems to be His favorite means of communicating with you?

List the traits and actions of the Son mentioned in these verses. How do these traits and actions compare to those of God? What do your findings imply about the relationship between Jesus and God?

Which of these traits or actions means the most to you today? Why?

> "God's glory is best seen in Jesus Christ. He, the Light of the world, illuminates God's nature. Because of Jesus, we are no longer in the dark about what God is really like."
>
> —Rick Warren

Read the sidebar quote by Rick Warren. Do you think he means

Jesus is God's last message? His best message? His ultimate message? Or His only self-revealing message? Justify your choice.

The author of Hebrews tells us the Son is seated at God's right hand in heaven. What does this imply about His rank and authority? What does it imply about His work of providing purification from sin? How does your relationship with Jesus reflect His rank in heaven? How has His work changed your life?

Meditate on Hebrews 1:5–14.

The author repeats the question "to which of the angels did God ever say . . .?" in Hebrews 1:5 and 13. What is the implied answer to these questions? Why do you think the author repeated the question with differing quotations? How does this question support his argument about the Son being superior to the angels?

What does God say about the angels in Hebrews 1:7? How is that different from what He says about the Son in Hebrews 1:8–12? What do these statements imply about Jesus?

Read what John Wesley wrote about angels in the sidebar at right. How does this statement compare to Hebrews 1:14? What are the implications about the relationship between angels and Christians?

> John Wesley wrote that angels minister before God and are "sent forth to attend to men."
>
> —Explanatory Notes on the New Testament

Why do you think angels and prophets might have been distracting to these Jewish Christians? Why would people be tempted to follow angels instead of Jesus?

What kinds of religious ideas or personalities can distract you from faithfully following Jesus? Why? How can you resist that temptation?

Meditate on Hebrews 2:1–4.

The author tells us "we must pay more careful attention" to the message Jesus brought. What is the peril of not paying attention?

What happened to those who ignored the angels' message? What is the implied answer to the question in Hebrews 2:3? How do you feel about the author using that kind of motivation in a call to pay close attention to Jesus? Why?

> "It was the will of God that we should have a sure footing for our faith, and a strong foundation for our hope in receiving the gospel."
>
> —Matthew Henry

The author indicates that Jesus delivered the message that demands close attention. Since only a few people met Him face to face, how can His message be confirmed to us? How has God testified to the authenticity of Jesus' message in your life?

Read Matthew Henry's quote in the sidebar above. In a world that believes all religions lead to God, what provides the foundation for your faith in Jesus? What keeps you from drifting away in the current of this so-called tolerance?

Read the sidebar observation about spiritual uncertainty. In what ways has God used insecurity and doubt to draw you into a deeper relationship with Jesus? What, if any, questions are you struggling with today?

"*Spiritual* uncertainty is like the silent red light on the instrument panel of an automobile. It flashes its warning to tell us the oil is low and there is imminent danger to the motor. Under these conditions the very lack of assurance for which our hearts hunger is one more of God's gifts of grace to us."

—A. F. Harper

CONTEMPLATION ✞ REFLECT AND YIELD

In what areas of your life do you need to pay more careful attention? Why?

How does the warning in this passage affect your desire to stand firm in your faith?

PRAYER ✝ RESPOND TO GOD

When and how did the message of Jesus bring salvation to you? Thank God for sending Jesus to purify you from sin. Listen for the Spirit's assurance of your salvation.

INCARNATION ✝ LIVE THE WORD

For five minutes each day this week, pay close attention to Jesus. Find a quiet place that's free of interruptions. Pray, "Speak Lord, for Your servant is listening." If distracting thoughts come, write them on a piece of paper and then return your attention to concentrating on hearing Jesus' instructions for you.

HE KNOWS MY PAIN

Listening for God through Hebrews 2:5–18

SUMMARY

This text will remind you of the heights of honor God created us to experience. It also will direct your attention to the lengths to which Jesus went in order to restore us. The Son of God did not sidestep any of the pain inherent to life in a fallen world. He took it all in.

The same Son introduced in Hebrews 1:1–4 as "the exact representation of God" became exactly like us. He experienced every part of life and death as a flesh and blood human being.

It's been said that the Son of God became human so human beings could become the children of God. These verses testify to the truth of that statement. Hebrews 2:5–18 will prompt you to believe that Jesus knows all about your sorrows. He was tempted so He can help you. Jesus suffered and died so He can identify with you in every way.

SILENCE ✝ LISTEN FOR GOD

Use your imagination to stand at the foot of Jesus' cross. Hear Him as He cries out, "My God, why have You forsaken me?" Listen for God's comforting declaration.

PREPARATION ✝ FOCUS YOUR THOUGHTS

Read Charles Wesley's comments on the crucifixion in the sidebar below.

When you contemplate the cross and God dying there for you, what are your thoughts and feelings? What does it motivate you to do?

> My Lord, my Love, is crucified! Is Crucified for me and you, To bring us rebels back to God; Believe, believe the record true, Ye all are bought with Jesus' blood; Pardon for all flows from His side; My Lord, my Love, is crucified!
>
> —Charles Wesley

READING ✝ HEAR THE WORD

Jesus became flesh/man -so —>

This passage is an explanation of David's awestruck response to God's creation, found in Psalm 8. God intended for humans to rule over His physical creation. He planned for our race to manage this world and to answer only to Him. Adam and Eve surrendered that place of honor to Satan when they sinned.

Jesus now takes over on man's behalf

As these verses continue to develop the author's argument that Jesus is superior to the angels, they show how He conquered Satan and restored fallen humanity by becoming one of us. He fulfilled humanity's role in ruling creation so the angels do not have dominion in God's kingdom. His identification with us is so complete that we have become His brothers and sisters.

You will find these terms in Hebrews 2:5–18.

World to come: These words refer to Christ's future reign in "a new heaven and a new earth" where "there will be no more death or mourning or crying or pain" (Rev. 21:1–4).

Grace: This refers to God giving to us something we do not deserve, cannot earn, and can never repay.

Make holy: This is sanctification. It is Christ's work in our lives that changes our inner being and then our behavior. It is everything God does to make us more like Jesus.

Atonement: This is the effect of a sacrifice in taking away both God's judgment and the sin that causes it.

MEDITATION ✝ ENGAGE THE WORD

Meditate on Hebrews 2:5–9.

Hebrews 2:6–8 quotes from Psalm 8. The Revised Standard Version translates Psalm 8:5 as, "Yet thou hast made him a little less that God." How does this view compare to your view of humankind?

Read the commentary on Psalm 8:5 in the sidebar. Do you see yourself as "puny and insignificant" or as a person bearing God's image with glory and royal authority? Why do you think as you do?

"Far from puny and insignificant, we have been made in God's image, crowned with His glory, and set over our own kingdom. Some object to this description. They warn against putting too much emphasis on human ability and observe that whatever glory humanity had at the beginning was lost in the Fall. While sin has considerably hampered progress, the description in Psalm 8 describes ... the son of man ... a term that refers to humankind outside the Garden of Eden."

—Stephen J. Lennox

The author of Hebrews writes that God has ranked humans right below Him. If God put everything under humankind, why is it that "we do not see everything subject" to us? Who is in control of this world now? Why?

Jesus stands in contrast to the rest of humanity. In what ways was Jesus made a little lower than the angels? What did He receive as a result of suffering and dying? What does the author imply when he writes that Jesus tasted death for everyone?

Read Philippians 2:5–11. How do those verses compare to the thoughts of Hebrews 2:5–9? In Philippians 2:5 we are commanded to have the same attitude as Jesus. How would you describe that attitude? How did Jesus view Himself? What was His motivation for becoming a human being? Why did He choose to die on the cross? If you had the same attitude toward God, toward yourself, and toward others as Jesus had, what would it mean in your life? What, if anything, would you need to change? How would you relate to God and others differently?

Meditate on Hebrews 2:10–13.

The word *glory* appears three times in Hebrews 2:5–10. The author of Hebrews said Jesus is "the radiance of God's glory" in Hebrews 1:3. Use a Bible dictionary to discover the meaning of this word. What does the meaning of *glory* imply about God's goal for you?

Read Hebrews 5:8, and compare it to Hebrews 2:10. What do they have in common?

Read John Piper's quote in the sidebar. How can you explain the fact that God made Jesus the author of our salvation through suffering? Do you think it is appropriate or right for us to benefit from Jesus' pain? What other meanings could this verse have? Would any of these alternatives make sense in this context? Why or why not?

> "When the Bible says that Jesus 'learned obedience through what he suffered,' it … means that with each new trial he learned in practice—and in pain—what it means to obey. When it says that he was 'made perfect through suffering,' it … means that he was gradually fulfilling the perfect righteousness that he had to have in order to save us."
>
> —John Piper

What does it mean to be holy? In what ways is God holy? In what ways was Jesus holy? In what ways are you holy? Talk about a time when you experienced Jesus' power to make you holy in some area of your life.

Paul often referred to himself a slave of Jesus Christ. Hebrews 2:11 declares that we are brothers and sisters with Jesus in God's family. What is the difference between a slave and a child? How do you feel about Jesus calling you brother or sister? What does being a sibling of Jesus imply about your relationships with other Christians?

> Incarnation is God's promise to be a committed participant with us in our living, our imagining, our dreaming, and our yearning.
> —W. Paul Jones

Meditate on Hebrews 2:14–18.

Jesus shared our humanity. God the Son became a flesh and blood man. Theologians call this unique event the Incarnation. Compare these verses with Colossians 2:13–15. How did Jesus destroy the devil? How did He set us free from the fear of death?

Read the above sidebar about the Incarnation. What would happen in your life if you were completely convinced that God would be a "committed participant" with you?

Do you really believe Jesus suffered when He was tempted? Do you think Jesus could help you in your temptations if He had not suffered through it Himself? Why or why not?

CONTEMPLATION † REFLECT AND YIELD

In which of your dreams and plans do you think God feels most free to participate? On which ones have you been flying solo? Surrender all of your dreams and plans to Jesus.

PRAYER † RESPOND TO GOD

Pray a sentence prayer aloud that welcomes God to join your everyday living, dreaming, and planning. Listen for His promise to be a committed participant with you.

INCARNATION † LIVE THE WORD

Verbally welcome Jesus to participate with you in the development of your to-do lists each day this week. Listen for God's guidance as you walk through your daily routine. Expect Him to be a committed partner in all your decisions.

I WILL OBEY

Listening for God through Hebrews 3:1–19

Epitome

SUMMARY

All the world's religions begin with the concept of separation. Whether it is separation from God the Creator or from a blissful spiritual state, we all want to know how to bridge the gap between where we are and where we want to be. The answer to that question is amazingly consistent in all religions except for Christianity. Most religions teach that obedience to a set of rules will bridge the gap. Disobedience to those rules only widens the breech.

In contrast to other religions, the message of Hebrews 3 declares that God bridged the gap through Jesus. Our response is simply to trust in His provision. Trust establishes our relationship with God. Then we obey out of love and faithfulness to our Father

God. So, as you will see, the key question for Christians is one of trust. Obedience will flow from the answer to that question.

SILENCE ✝ LISTEN FOR GOD

Read Psalm 139:23–24 silently and prayerfully. Listen for the Spirit's encouragement and conviction as He searches your life.

PREPARATION ✝ FOCUS YOUR THOUGHTS

Think back to your childhood. Would your parents describe you as a strong-willed child? Tell about a time when you refused to do what you were told.

READING ✝ HEAR THE WORD

Hebrews was written to encourage Jewish believers to remain faithful to Jesus despite persecution and trials. The author opens Hebrews by describing Jesus in terms that reveal His divinity. Then he calls us to pay careful attention to Jesus' message in order to avoid drifting away.

In Hebrews 3 the author calls his readers to focus on Jesus. He warns them of the danger of unbelief and unfaithfulness. Hebrews 3 cites the rebellion of the Israelites when they refused to enter the Promised Land (Numbers 14). Those people did not believe God could or would help them possess the land, so they refused to go in.

The author states twice that what Jesus has done for us is conditional. If we hold on to our hope and if we hold firmly until the end, we will share in His glory. We need to encourage each other to remain resolute.

The following terms are keys to understanding this passage.

Faithful: A faithful person trusts God or is filled with faith in Him. The concept also implies that the faithful person acts in a trustworthy, dependable manner.

Hope: This is our confident expectation of all God has promised in Jesus.

Unbelief: This is the opposite of faith. An unbelieving person does not trust God and so refuses to obey Him.

MEDITATION ✝ ENGAGE THE WORD

Meditate on Hebrews 3:1–6.

Jesus is God's Son. He became a human to suffer and die for everyone. He has destroyed the Devil and set us free from the fear of death. He has brought us into God's family, so we must "fix [our] thoughts on Jesus." Why would the author call for this application of Hebrews 1 and 2? How would this assist his readers?

Jesus is called *Apostle* and *High Priest*. What kind of ministry does each of these titles imply? How do they encourage you to focus on Jesus?

Make a chart to compare Jesus to Moses. How are they like each other? How are they different? Why was this comparison made? How would it encourage faithfulness?

Jesus built God's house. What is the condition for being included in God's house? *Believing in Jesus as our Savior, High priest & King + Gods word*

In what situations have you been tempted to let go of your hope in Jesus? How have you managed to maintain a firm grasp of your courage in those times?

Meditate on Hebrews 3:7–15.

Since there is a condition for receiving God's promises, we must not make the mistake of those who rebelled against God. They heard His command to enter the Promised Land but refused to go in. What happened to Israel when they rebelled? In your opinion what is implied by the phrase "harden your hearts"? How would you describe your heart today? Why?

Read Numbers 14 and Psalm 95. How do these Old Testament passages illustrate the need to hold firm to our faith? How can you explain the fact that the ones who refused to enter the Promised Land had seen the plagues in Egypt, walked through the Red Sea on dry ground, and heard God's thundering voice at Mount Sinai?

Read the quote about sin in the sidebar. Do you agree with this definition? Why? How does it compare to what the author of Hebrews says about unbelief and sin?

"Sin is ... the unwillingness of man to acknowledge his ... dependence upon God and his effort to make his own life independent and secure."

—Reinhold Niebuhr

Hebrews 3:12–13 indicates that the antidote for unbelief, sin, and hard hearts is found in an encouraging fellowship. Have you ever turned away from the living God to build your own independent life? What were the results? Did a fellow believer help you back? If so, how? What recommendations would you make to someone wanting to encourage a wandering brother or sister?

Read the statement by Rick Warren in the sidebar. What part should God's family play in encouraging your faithfulness? Can you share an example of a time when you either gave or received encouragement?

"'Mind your own business' is not a Christian phrase. We are called and commanded to be involved in each other's lives."

—Rick Warren

There is a condition for sharing in Christ and His blessings. What must you do to participate in the blessings Jesus came to give?

Meditate on Hebrews 3:16–19.

Read the sidebar at right about obedience. In what ways was Israel's rebellion a moment of truth for the nation? What was

"In many ways, obedience is your moment of truth. What you do will: (1) Reveal what you believe about Him. (2) Determine whether you will experience His might in and through you. (3) Determine whether you come to know Him more intimately."

—Henry Blackaby and Claude King

the result of their disobedience? What did their disobedience reveal about their view of God? Have you ever thought of your decisions in this way? How will this concept of belief generating obedience shape your future choices?

CONTEMPLATION ✝ REFLECT AND YIELD

Think back over the last two weeks. When was your most recent moment of truth? Did you trust and obey? If you did, thank God for His help. Did you disobey? If you did, confess your sin and receive His cleansing forgiveness.

PRAYER ✝ RESPOND TO GOD

Find a prayer partner to discuss any areas where you struggle to trust God enough to obey Him. Intercede for each other. Listen for Jesus' voice of gentle encouragement.

INCARNATION ✝ LIVE THE WORD

Do you know a discouraged and wandering Christian? Pray for him or her every day this week. Look for an opportunity to minister to that person.

I ENJOY GOD'S PRESENCE

Listening for God through Hebrews 4:1–16

SUMMARY

Israel had been refused entrance into the Promised Land because of unbelief. Hebrews 3:18–19 points out that the people failed to enter God's *rest*. Beginning there and continuing through most of chapter 4, the author uses the word *rest* in three ways. The first way denotes the Promised Land along with its liberation from oppression and freedom to worship the Lord. The second use indicates the Sabbath Day established by God at the end of Creation. Both of these uses are illustrations of the third use, which signifies the freedom from sin Jesus alone can provide. It includes the liberty to enjoy His presence as we live and worship. The fullest experience of this rest will be found in heaven. However, you will discover that you can enjoy God's rest in increasing measure here and now.

SILENCE ✝ LISTEN FOR GOD

Slowly whisper this prayer three or four times. "Lord Jesus, have mercy on me a sinner." Listen for His pardoning voice.

PREPARATION ✝ FOCUS YOUR THOUGHTS

When do you feel closest to God? How is this time different from other times?

Where do you go to find peace? What makes that place special?

Finish this sentence: "I feel most comfortable with God ..."

READING ✝ HEAR THE WORD

The following words and phrases are important in Hebrews 4.

Gospel: The good news of God's promised blessings. In this passage it applies to both Old Testament and New Testament promises.

Joshua: The successor to Moses who led Israel into the Promised Land forty years after the rebellion. *Jesus* is the Greek form of *Joshua.* So the author contrasts Joshua the Old Testament hero with Joshua the Son of God.

Throne of grace: The center of God's power and authority where He gives His blessings to undeserving people.

Mercy: This is forgiveness for all sins.

MEDITATION ✝ ENGAGE THE WORD

Meditate on Hebrews 4:1–5.

Israel refused to enter God's rest, but God's offer is still open. So the author calls readers to make sure they, too, do not fall short of His rest. What similarities are there between the gospel we have heard and the gospel Israel heard before its rebellion? Why did the message they heard fail to be of value to them? What will happen if you have faith in the gospel you've heard?

Read Genesis 2:1–3. What is the relationship between the rest refused by Israel, the rest of God on the seventh day, and the rest that remains for the believer?

Meditate on Hebrews 4:6–11.

The people of Israel heard God's message but did not combine it with faith. They disobeyed His command, and they missed out on His rest. But some will still enter today.

How is this open promise of rest encouraging to you? What benefits do you expect to experience should you enter God's rest? What kind of work will you rest from? Is it the work of trying to earn His acceptance and approval? If so, why can you rest from it?

> "Having committed my all to God, I rest. He cares for me. No final harm can come to me while I lean back on Him."
> —A. F. Harper

Read A. F. Harper's statement in the sidebar. What does he consider the key to entering God's rest? Have you committed your all to God and His loving care? If not, what seems to hinder you from doing so? In what ways are you struggling to trust God to care for you?

The Amplified New Testament puts Hebrews 4:11 like this: "Let us therefore be zealous *and* exert ourselves *and* strive diligently to enter into that rest [of God]—to know and experience it for ourselves." What level of priority do the words *zealous, exert,* and *strive diligently* seem to convey? Is knowing and experiencing God's rest a high priority to you? Or is it merely an interesting topic for discussion in a Bible study? What would happen if you made entering God's rest your top priority?

The goal of entering God's rest is to keep everyone from disobedience. Do you think of the Christian life as an individual endeavor or a team effort? What are the pros and cons of each point of view?

Meditate on Hebrews 4:12–16.

To truly experience God's rest takes effort, because we cannot fake our way into it. God's Word will not allow it. In what ways is the Word of God "living and active"? What can the Word of God accomplish that prevents hypocrisy? Tell about a time when your thoughts and attitudes were exposed by God's Word.

In Psalm 139:7–18 the psalmist draws consolation from God's uninterrupted presence in his life. Are you comforted by the idea that no part of you life is hidden from God? How does knowing He sees everything about you affect your decisions and behavior? Why?

List the unique qualifications of Jesus that make Him our Great High Priest. Which one makes Him seem most accessible to you? Why?

"On the way to the cross for thirty years, Christ was tempted like every human is tempted. True, he never sinned. But wise people have pointed out that this means His temptations were stronger than ours, not weaker."

—John Piper

Read the sidebar quote about Jesus' temptations. How is resisting temptation without sinning more difficult than eventually giving in to it? What temptations do you find are a constant battle? What would you expect from someone who was victorious over the temptations you struggle with often? What does Jesus promise?

Read A. W. Tozer's statement in the sidebar. Do you believe God's mercy is available for every weakness, mistake, and sin in your life? Do you feel free to enter His presence boldly and joyfully? Explain your answer.

"To receive mercy we must first know that God is merciful. And it is not enough to believe that He once showed mercy to Noah or Abraham or David and will again show mercy in some future happy day. We must believe that God's mercy is boundless, free and, through Jesus Christ our Lord, available to us now in our present situation."

—A. W. Tozer

CONTEMPLATION
✝ REFLECT AND YIELD

Is there an attitude or habit that you feel uncomfortable about in Jesus' presence? Are you willing to admit that to Him? Will you surrender it and receive His mercy and grace?

PRAYER ✝ RESPOND TO GOD

Meditate on this song lyric: *Just as I am, You will welcome and receive*. Listen for God's loving voice as He welcomes you home.

INCARNATION ✝ LIVE THE WORD

As you begin your daily time alone with God each day this week, meditate on these words: *Just as I am, You will welcome and receive*. Repeat it aloud as a prayer, and enjoy God's presence.

I Am Completely Saved

Listening for God through Hebrews 7:11–28

Summary

The Holiest Place in the Temple was the inner room. It was considered God's throne room on earth. Gentiles could not enter the Temple itself. Jewish women were relegated to a courtyard. Jewish men could go into an area a little closer to the holiest place. The priests were the only ones allowed in the area surrounding the holiest place. But access to that inner room was granted only to the high priest on one day each year.

Jesus is our Great High Priest. He supercedes the priesthood of the Old Testament system, because He accomplished what it could not. Jesus took away all the guilt and penalty of sin. He removed that barrier between God and us. He ushers everyone who believes in Him into heaven's throne room.

You will not be excluded when you come to Him by faith. As you study, you will find a deep assurance. Jesus saves you completely.

SILENCE ✝ LISTEN FOR GOD

Silently repeat one or two of Jesus' titles, such as *High Priest* or *Savior*, several times. Listen for God to call you, "My child."

PREPARATION ✝ FOCUS YOUR THOUGHTS

If you could change one thing about your past, what would it be? How would that change affect you now? Explain your reasons for wanting this change.

READING ✝ HEAR THE WORD

The author of Hebrews has asserted that you were created to enjoy God's presence, but sin prevents that from happening. So Jesus became the Great High Priest. By experiencing all of life's temptations and pain, culminating in His death on a cross, Jesus opened the promise of resting in God's presence to everyone.

These assertions would have raised questions in the mind of his Jewish audience. God established the Levitical priesthood. Each priest had to prove he was a direct descendant of Aaron, the first high priest. The sacrificial system at the Temple had remained in effect for more than a thousand years. Jesus was not a descendant of Aaron. How could Jesus be the Great High Priest? Why would God change the very system He had instituted?

The author answers these questions in Hebrews 7:11–28.

You will encounter these terms in this text.

Perfect: We tend to think of *perfect* as meaning *flawless, faultless,* or *unspoiled.* However, in the Bible *perfect* and its various forms refer to a person or thing that accomplishes the purpose for which it was intended. For example, a hammer is perfect for driving nails; but even a flawless hammer is not perfect for stirring cake batter.

Melchizedek: A non-Jewish priest of God to whom Abraham paid a tithe (Genesis 14:18–20 and Hebrews 7:1–10).

Meditatio

MEDITATION ✝ ENGAGE THE WORD

Meditate on Hebrews 7:11–17.

The Levitical priesthood could not realize "perfect fellowship between God and the worshipper" (AMP). Therefore, a new priest and a new order were necessary. We need a priest who can lead us into God's presence with confidence and joy.

Read Hebrews 7:1–10. How are Melchizedek and Jesus similar? How are they different? In what ways are they superior to the Levitical priesthood?

How would you describe perfect fellowship with God to a young child?

Read the quote from Barclay in the sidebar. If the goal of religion is free access to God, what barriers did the Levitical priesthood fail to remove? What limited the effectiveness of those priests? Would you have been satisfied with the end result of their ritual?

> "As we read this passage we have to remember the basic idea of religion which never leaves the mind of the writer to the Hebrews. To him religion is access to God's presence as friends, with nothing between us and Him."
>
> —William Barclay

Find and examine a diagram of the Temple in Jerusalem. Who had access to God's presence? How close to the holiest place would you have been able to go?

Why do you suppose the holiest place was off limits to almost everyone? Read Matthew 27:50–51. What does that imply about the whole system of laws and rituals surrounding the Temple?

Meditate on Hebrews 7:18–22.

Draw a chart to compare the priests—Melchizedek, Aaron, and Jesus. Compare and contrast their ancestries, their descendents, their life expectancies, and how their priesthoods were established. What similarities do you see? What differences? Why are the differences significant?

In what ways did the law fail? Have you tried to gain access to God's presence through your own good deeds and religious acts? What caused you to realize the futility of that effort? Have you found peace in God's presence through Jesus? Share your story.

Meditate on Hebrews 7:23–28.

What prevented other priests from continuing in office? Why isn't Jesus limited in the same way? What is the result of Jesus' ministry as our priest? Are you comforted and encouraged by the stability of Jesus' priesthood? Why?

> "Christ has the power to save us completely and perfectly. He can save us not only from the guilt and punishment of sin, but also from its nature and power."
>
> —A. F. Harper

Read the statement by A. F. Harper in the sidebar. What are some reasons he might believe that? What difference does it make in terms of your security with God that Jesus "is able to save completely"? How does it affect your daily decisions and activities? What does it do to your desire to follow Jesus? Why?

Read George Buttrick's sidebar statement about intercession. Do you believe Jesus' intercession for you is both specific and pondered? Does Jesus bear your burden in His heart? How would it make you feel if you could hear His prayers for you? Explain.

> "Intercession is more that just specific, it is pondered; it requires us to bear on our heart the burden of those for whom we pray."
>
> —George Buttrick

According to Hebrews 7:26-28, what can Jesus do that no other priest can do? What character qualities set Him apart from Levitical priests? How is His sacrifice superior to theirs? Why was Jesus' sacrifice a "once for all" event? Of what benefit to you is that?

Summarize the author's argument for the superiority of Jesus' priesthood. Make this your own personal statement. Begin by finishing this sentence. "Jesus is the only priest who can meet my needs, because ..."

CONTEMPLATION ✟ REFLECT AND YIELD

What old ways tempt you to turn away from Jesus? How is He better than those old ways?

PRAYER ✟ RESPOND TO GOD

Is there an area of your life where you struggle to earn God's acceptance and approval? Why have you found it hard to entrust this into Jesus' hands? Pray through these reasons until you know you are completely saved in this area of life.

Incarnation ✝ Live the Word

Each day this week, quiet yourself before God and listen for Him to say, "Your sins are completely forgiven."

I AM HIS AND
HE IS MINE

Listening for God through Hebrews 8:1–13; 9:11–15

SUMMARY

Jesus established a new covenant between God and humans with His sacrifice on the cross. This agreement with God promises to clear our consciences of guilt and shame. The Old Testament sacrifices provided atonement, or covering, for sin. This made individuals ritually clean so they could fellowship with God. However the sin, along with its guilt and shame, remained. Their consciences were not clean.

The New Covenant, brought by Jesus, moves us into an intimate relationship with God. The covenant with Israel was based on obedience to the Law. The rebellious attitude common to all humans prevented the Israelites from keeping the covenant, so they did not experience intimacy with God.

As you study the New Covenant you will discover that Jesus can change that rebellious attitude and write the law of love on your heart. You will experience the thrill of knowing that you are His and He is yours.

SILENCE ✝ LISTEN FOR GOD

Imagine the Holy Spirit flowing around and through your soul like a crystal-clear river. Allow Him to wash away any guilt you have. Listen for God's approval and acceptance.

PREPARATION ✝ FOCUS YOUR THOUGHTS

What conditions are set for an intimate marriage in the wedding vows?

After a wedding, can a couple honestly say they belong to each other? Why?

How does the relationship of a married couple change over time?

In what ways might your relationship with God change over time?

READING ✦ HEAR THE WORD

Human beings were created for an intimate relationship with God. However, sin separated us from Him. Even so, he Lord promised the Israelites that He would walk among them; He would be their God, and they would be His people if they obeyed His commands. For hundreds of years, Israel assumed that the Temple fulfilled that promise. However, the destruction of Jerusalem in 587 B.C. brought that to an end.

The prophets Jeremiah, Ezekiel, Joel, and Zechariah stirred up Israel's hunger for this intimate relationship once again. God repeatedly promised to change His people from the inside out. For example, Ezekiel 11:19–20 says, "I will give them an undivided heart and put a new spirit in them; I will remove from them their heart of stone and give them a heart of flesh. Then they will follow my decrees and be careful to keep my laws. They will be my people, and I will be their God." The prophet Jeremiah says something similar in the passage quoted by the writer to the Hebrews in this text.

The following are key terms to understand in this passage.

*C*ovenant: This is an agreement voluntarily entered by two parties. God sets the conditions for gaining access to His presence. All persons who meet those conditions will be His people, and He will be their God.

*M*ediator: A person who negotiates and institutes agreements between two parties.

MEDITATION ✝ ENGAGE THE WORD

Meditate on Hebrews 8:1~7.

Review Hebrews 7:26. What makes Jesus the high priest we need? In this section of Hebrews 8, what two descriptions does the author add in regard to Jesus?

Is Jesus the only person who can function as the high priest we need? Has any other religious leader met the same qualifications? How would you communicate this truth to someone of a different religion?

How are the places, structures, and assignments of the two priesthoods contrasted in these verses? Why did Moses need to follow God's pattern for the Tabernacle precisely?

Reflect on your own patterns of worship. In what ways do they reflect worship in heaven's sanctuary?

Meditate on Hebrews 8:7–13.

If the goal of the first covenant was to restore the relationship between God and humans, why was a new covenant needed? What was the fault in the first one? In your opinion, why didn't God start with the second covenant?

What was God's reason for establishing a different covenant? List the blessings you can receive in the new covenant. Rank them in the order of what seems most helpful to you at this time. Explain your position.

Read the commitment prayer from John Wesley's *Covenant Service* in the sidebar. What are the implications for each of the promises Wesley called the early Methodists to make?

I am no longer my own, but Yours. Put me to what You will, rank me with whom You will; put me to doing, put me to suffering; let me be employed for You or laid aside for You, praised for You or humbled for You; let me be full, let me be empty; let me have all things, let me have nothing; I freely and cheerfully yield all things to Your pleasure and disposal.

–John Wesley

What possible changes might you see God make in your life if you pray these promises? How do you feel about the idea of giving God full authority in your life? Why?

Read Matthew Henry's statement in the sidebar, and compare it to Jesus' words in Luke 22:19–20. Have you been baptized? What kinds of promises and commitments are made in a baptismal service? Do you find Communion to be a time of renewal and commitment? Why?

> "The articles of this covenant ... are sealed between God and His people by baptism and the Lord's Supper; whereby they bind themselves to their part, and God assures them He will do His part; and His is the main and principle part, on which His people depend for grace and strength to do theirs."
>
> —Matthew Henry

Meditate on Hebrews 9:11–15.

Where does Jesus carry out his priestly duties? How did He gain entrance to the tabernacle? Does the phrase "once for all" refer to all persons? All sins? All time? All believers? Something else? Give reasons for your choice.

What did the blood and ashes of animals accomplish for the Israelites? What can Jesus' blood do for us?

Read Piper's quote in the sidebar. Have you ever experienced a guilty conscience and found relief in Jesus' blood? Share your story.

"When our conscience rises up and condemns us, where will we turn? We turn to Christ. We turn to the suffering and death of Christ—the blood of Christ. This is the only cleansing agent in the universe that can give the conscience relief in life and peace in death."

—John Piper

The author of Hebrews used Old Testament images and rituals to convince believing Jews to remain faithful to Jesus. How would you explain Jesus' death to a non-religious person? What images would you use? Why?

How do you feel about this emphasis on blood and sacrifices? Why does God insist on establishing His covenants with blood?

How does the fact that the new covenant has replaced the old, obsolete covenant play out in your life? Does it form the foundation for your relationship with God? If so, is it a foundation you take for granted or one that increases in value to you in the storms of life? Please explain.

CONTEMPLATION ✝ REFLECT AND YIELD

Reflect on the changes God might call you to make in response to Wesley's covenant prayer. List any and all of your qualms, and surrender them to Jesus as you pray, "I am yours, and you are mine."

PRAYER ✝ RESPOND TO GOD

Reread John Wesley's covenant prayer in the sidebar on page 55. Think about the changes it might call you to make. Listen for the Spirit's invitation to surrender your life to God.

INCARNATION ✝ LIVE THE WORD

Pray the Lord's Prayer each day this week. Emphasize the following statement in your heart: "Your will be done."

I HAVE COME TO
DO YOUR WILL

Listening for God through Hebrews 10:1~18

SUMMARY

Jesus set the standard for submitting to God's will. One facet of the mystery of the Incarnation is that Jesus had freedom of choice exactly as we do. He was God, so He was in agreement with God's plan. At the same time, He was a human being with a free will that He needed to surrender to God's purpose.

Jesus learned to be obedient to His parents (Luke 2:51). Then in the Garden of Gethsemane, He surrendered His will to the Father's (Luke 22:42). Paul tells us in Philippians 2:8 that Jesus "became obedient to death—even death on a cross!" The author of Hebrews sums up Jesus' submissive attitude with the words "Here I am, I have come to do your will."

Jesus' sacrifice on the cross makes us perfect while it makes us holy. As we follow in His footsteps, we learn to submit our will to God's will. As we do this, we discover both the necessity of and the peace that follows surrendering to God's will.

SILENCE ✝ LISTEN FOR GOD

Imagine Jesus praying in the Garden. Contemplate His struggles. Listen for Jesus' voice saying, "I did it for you."

PREPARATION ✝ FOCUS YOUR THOUGHTS

Jesus prayed "Not my will but yours be done" three times. Why did God's Son need to pray this prayer? Why did He pray it more than once? Describe a time when you needed to pray this same prayer.

READING ✝ HEAR THE WORD

The Trinity is seen working for our salvation in these verses. Hebrews 10:1–10 outlines God the Father's will for our salvation and sanctification through Jesus' sacrifice. Hebrews 10:11–14 points out how God the Son made the final sacrifice that makes us holy. Hebrews 10:15–18 describes God the Spirit's work in changing our hearts and reprogramming our minds.

There are two key phrases in this part of Hebrews.

Make perfect: In this context, to make someone perfect is to help him or her become and do what God intended.

Make holy: This phrase also can be translated *sanctify.* It is everything God does to make us more like Jesus. Sanctification makes us more like God designed us to be. At the same time, it makes us more like God.

MEDITATION ✞ ENGAGE THE WORD

Meditate on Hebrews 10:1–4.

The law and rituals of the first covenant were unable to meet our need. They could not make us what God had intended for us to be. According to Hebrews 10:1, what was the reason for their inadequacy? How does the endless repetition of the sacrifices prove they cannot make us what God intended us to be?

Observe a shadow for a minute or two. What can you learn about the reality behind it by watching the shadow? In what ways does the law shadow the sacrifice of Jesus?

Why couldn't the blood of animals take away our sins? How would you have felt if you had been reminded of your sins year after year without ever receiving release from your guilt? What would you have wanted to do? Why?

Meditate on Hebrews 10:5–10.

The author draws a contrast between sacrifices and Jesus' statement, "Here I am, I have come to do your will." How many reasons can you think of for God to desire Jesus' obedience more than animal sacrifices? What does this imply about your submission to God's will and your religious acts?

According to Hebrews 10:10, what was God's will? How are holiness and obedience connected? Are you holy because of your submission to the Father or because of Jesus' doing God's will? In other words, are you holy because of what you do or because of what Jesus did? Explain the difference and the reasons for your answer.

Read the C. S. Lewis quote in the sidebar on page 63. Do you agree or disagree? Why? How would you summarize the central doctrine of Christianity? Would you be able to communicate it to a non-Christian? What would you say and why?

Meditate on Hebrews 10:11–18.

Use a chart to list the points of contrast between the animal sacrifices and Jesus' sacrifice. What would these differences mean to Jewish believers thinking about turning away from Jesus? What would turning away from Him result in?

> "The central Christian belief is that Christ's death has somehow put us right with God and given us a fresh start."
>
> —C. S. Lewis

Read the statement at right about Jesus' sacrifice in the sidebar at right. If Jesus is the final sacrifice for your sins, why do you need to submit your will to God? Explain your answer.

Hebrews 10:14 might be paraphrased this way: "By His one sacrifice on the cross, Jesus has made us what God intended for us to be as long as we are becoming more and more like Him." In what sense has Jesus made you what God planned for you? In what ways is He still in the process of changing you from the inside out?

> [Jesus] became the final Priest and the final Sacrifice. Sinless, He did not offer sacrifices for Himself. Immortal, He never has to be replaced. Human, He could bear human sins. Therefore, He did not offer sacrifices for himself; He offered himself as the final sacrifice."
>
> —John Piper

Read the quote by John Piper in the sidebar at right. Are you encouraged by your "experienced progress"? Why or why not? How is God inviting you to grow deeper in holiness?

Read the sidebar message taken from a church sign. How would you help an individual who knows the history of Jesus' death but not the salvation it provides? What recommendations would you make to help him recognize his need and the way to move into a relationship with Jesus?

> "Being sanctified means that we are imperfect and in process. We are becoming holy—but we are not yet fully holy. And it is precisely these—and only these—who are already perfected. The joyous encouragement here is that the evidence of our perfection before God is not our experienced perfection, but our experienced progress."
>
> —John Piper

> Jesus died on the cross—that's history. Jesus died for me— that's salvation.
>
> —A Church Sign

CONTEMPLATION ✝ REFLECT AND YIELD

Jesus submitted to the Father's will to demonstrate God's love to us sinners. To whom is the Father sending you to share His love? What act of kindness do they need? Will you do it?

PRAYER ✝ RESPOND TO GOD

Pray Jesus' prayer found in this text: "Here I am, I have come to do your will." Listen for the Spirit's voice to give you an assignment.

INCARNATION ✝ LIVE THE WORD

Each time you enter a building over the next seven days, pray, "Here I am, I have come to do your will." Watch for and seize opportunities to demonstrate God's love to someone.

I WILL WORSHIP

Listening for God through Hebrews 12:14–29

SUMMARY

Too often battle lines are drawn over the style of music or the Bible translation a congregation will use. These disputes usually miss the essence of worshipping God. It is *whom* we worship and not *how* we worship that counts.

Worship is a lifestyle of love—a life of obedience to the two great commandments (Mark 12:28–31). It is a growing holiness that is so focused on Jesus and on what others need that it gladly sacrifices its preferences for them. We worship best when we love God with all that we are and have while loving our neighbor as ourselves.

The pursuit of peace and holiness is a necessity for every Christian. In these verses, you will take notice of a call to worship the Lord in the beauty of holiness.

SILENCE ✝ LISTEN FOR GOD

Express your love to God silently, and quietly accept His embrace of love in return.

PREPARATION ✝ FOCUS YOUR THOUGHTS

Complete these sentences one by one.

"I worship best at …" (a place).

"I worship best when…" (a time).

"I enjoy worship music that …" (a style).

"I used to think worship was … but now I realize it is …" (a purpose).

READING ✝ HEAR THE WORD

Read Hebrews 12:14–29. These terms will be important to know as you listen to this passage.

Make every effort: The King James version translates this as *follow* while other translations say *strive for.* The idea involves running hard to reach a goal. Paul uses this concept in Philippians 3:12 and 14 to compare the Christian life to a track race.

Peace: We often think of peace as the absence of trouble, but in the Bible it is far more. It is everything that contributes to human well being. It grows out of living in obedience to God's principles (Prov. 3:1–2).

Holiness: This is an important attribute of God, but we can achieve it only in relative terms. God is absolutely holy, and we can become holy by being in His presence. Holiness will make us different from and separated from the world. We will learn to think, act, and relate to others as Jesus does.

Godless: This describes a person with no awareness of or interest in God. He or she is focused only on life in this world.

MEDITATION ✝ ENGAGE THE WORD

Meditate on Hebrews 12:14–17.

The author commands readers to run hard to reach two goals. What are the goals we are to strive to reach? Based on the definitions above, what actions might be involved in making every effort to attain them?

Read the quote by John Stott in the sidebar. Have you conceived of the Christian life as he does? How would you describe the life of following Jesus? Brainstorm ways to illustrate this principle of commitment and maturation.

List the four things the writer of Hebrews says we should avoid. Compare these four things to avoid with the two goals we are to pursue. How are they different? How does this set of warnings relate to those you've seen before in Hebrews (2:1–4; 3:12–4:2; 5:11–6:8; 10:26-31)? Which one speaks to your heart most clearly? Why?

> "You become a Christian in a moment, but not a mature Christian. Christ can enter, cleanse, and forgive you in a matter of seconds, but it will take much longer for your character to be transformed and molded to His will. ... When we receive Christ, a moment of commitment will lead to a lifetime of adjustment."
>
> —John Stott

K. P. Yohannan refers to "cheap grace"—forgiveness without lifestyle changes—in the sidebar on page 71. Do you agree that most Christians are not living lives that honor Jesus? What evidence can you share to support your answer?

Read the story of Jacob and Esau in Genesis 25. How does Esau's decision to trade his inheritance rights for food illustrate the things we need to avoid? Read Genesis 27. Why couldn't Esau inherit Isaac's blessing? What are the implications of this illustration regarding those who turn away from Jesus?

In your opinion, which of the instructions given in Hebrews 12:14–17 is most relevant for Christians today? For what reasons? Which one do you need to heed today?

"The Bible says that the only way to see the face of the Living God is to be pure and to be purged from sin in our heart. This is the fact that is lost in the 'cheap grace' gospel that has flooded our churches. And today, we are seeing the terrible fruit of this watered-down perversion of the truth —the world has swallowed the church. Most Christians are living carnal lives of defeat and failure."

–K. P. Yohannan

Meditate on Hebrews 12:18–24.

Draw a chart to contrast and compare the two mountains described in these verses. What is different about them? What is similar? What reasons for staying faithful to Jesus can be found in this contrast?

Meditate on Hebrews 12:25–29.

To whom must we listen? What will happen if we don't listen to Him? What will happen if we do? Which of these—the negative or the positive—is most motivating to you? Why?

What has God promised to do to the universe? What will happen to everything that cannot be shaken? What are we receiving? What does the author conclude about what we should do? How are we to respond to God's blessing? How can we worship God acceptably?

What examples of a "consuming fire" can you think of? Have you ever been near such a fire? What did it feel like? What was left behind after the fire passed?

In your opinion, why is God a consuming fire? Is it because of His holiness, His love, or another attribute? Justify your answer.

> "To become a disciple means a decisive and irrevocable turning to both God and neighbor. What follows from there is a journey which never ends in this life, a journey of continually discovering new dimensions of loving God and neighbor."
>
> —David J. Bosch

Read David Bosch's quote in the sidebar on the preceding page. Do you agree or disagree with Bosch's comment? How does this idea compare to the principles you've uncovered in Hebrews? Have you made "a decisive and irrevocable" turn toward God and others? Tell how the Holy Spirit brought you to the place where you made that decision. If you have not made that kind of turn toward God and your neighbor, what is holding you back? Can someone help you over the hump? If so, how?

CONTEMPLATION ✝ REFLECT AND YIELD

Have you decided to keep on learning to love God and your neighbor? How has this commitment guided your thoughts about worship? Are you willing to surrender your preferences to help others connect with God?

PRAYER ✝ RESPOND TO GOD

Silently invite the Holy Spirit to coach you on your pursuit of peace and holiness. Listen for His encouragement and correction as He shows you how to make a greater effort to reach these goals.

INCARNATION ✝ LIVE THE WORD

Pray the following prayer this week each time you start to study your Bible or prepare your heart for a worship service: "Lord Jesus, reveal a new dimension of loving my God and my neighbor to me now. I will worship You with my life."